Less Is More

Less Is More

Meditations on Simplicity, Balance, and Real Abundance

Mina Parker

PHOTOGRAPHS BY DANIEL TALBOTT

Conari Press

First published in 2009 by Conari Press,

an imprint of Red Wheel/Weiser, LLC

With offices at:

500 Third Street, Suite 230

San Francisco, CA 94107

www.redwheelweiser.com

Library of Congress Cataloging-in-Publication Data

Parker, Mina.

  Less is more : meditations on simplicity, balance, and focus / Mina Parker.

    p. cm.

  ISBN 978-1-57324-453-4 (alk. paper)

  1. Voluntary simplicity movement. 2. Simplicity. 3. Self-management. 4. Optimism. I. Title.

  BJ1496.P37 2009

  179'.9--dc22

                   2009010090

Cover and interior design by Maija Tollefson

Typeset in Joanna

Cover photograph © Daniel Talbott

Printed in Hong Kong

SS

10 9 8 7 6 5 4 3 2 1

6

Introduction

one

8

Hidden Treasures

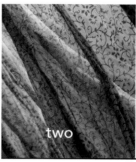

two

38

Enough Is Enough

three

68

What You See Is What You Get

four

96

Credit Where Credit Is Due

Introduction

'Tis the gift to be simple, 'tis the gift to be free,
'Tis the gift to come down where you ought to be,
And when we find ourselves in the place just right,
'Twill be in the valley of love and delight.

— ELDER JOSEPH BRACKETT

What a wonderful thing it would be to live in the world of this song—simple, free, and nestled into just the right place. We long for simplicity, we strive for freedom. Yet most of us feel a little (or a lot) worried. Our lives are anything but simple. They are hectic, overworked, overcomplicated. We feel anything but free; we are prisoners to our obligations, our fears, and our stress levels. Whether these sensations are old, familiar preoccupations, or hitting us with a new intensity in uncertain and difficult times, there's no time like the present to figure out how to feel better, and soon. There's no better moment to pack your bags and take the first steps toward that valley of love and delight, which can be found right here and right now.

But how? Our circumstances force us into a corner, and things seem to be getting worse and worse. Everything's shrinking—our budgets, our resources, our hope. The only things growing seem to be the mounting pile of debts and our fear of the unknown. Is there any comfort to be had? Is there any way to live the good life in an environment of scarcity?

Yes, there is. We only have to remember that in all sorts of situations, less really can be more. We can embrace simplicity as a desired outcome rather than a hardship we can't control. We can understand that our outlook, our attitude, and our ability to see the glass as being half full, again and again, day after day, is the key to our happiness. We can seek out comfort by remembering that all of this is meant to be, that hardships are life's best teachers, and that suffering is a temporary state. We can regain our footing and find our balance by recognizing that shadows ultimately define and enrich the brightest days. We can throw ourselves into new creation and transform our circumstances into new opportunities by embracing a credo of recycling and renewal. Most of all, we can give back and move forward through a daily practice of gratitude and the intense joy it brings us. We can do all this by embracing the power of Less Is More, and I hope the meditations and the images in this book will comfort and inspire you on your path to finding true simplicity, balance, and abundance.

one

Hidden Treasures

Savoring Simplicity and Cultivating Clarity

Imagine you found a map hidden away in a dusty corner of the attic. It has all the requisite attributes: yellowed parchment, fraying edges, and a big red X marking the spot. Hidden treasure, and only you know how to find it. If you found that map at the age of thirteen you would step right into that adventure, doing everything in your power to find the cache of gold. If you found it today, would you do the same? I hope so.

In our adult lives we're always on the lookout for what can feel like more elusive treasures: extra time, extra money, a chance to make a better life for ourselves and our children. We already have the map, though we may have lost it momentarily in some secret back room of our psyche. The X sits squarely over the life we want to lead, the life that is free for the taking if we only take the time to find it.

To follow the paces toward that hidden treasure in our everyday lives, all we have to do is rediscover the wonders of clarity and the rewards of simplicity. Step by step, we can easily reclaim the good life through a renewed attention to the little things that matter most. Once found and claimed, that's a treasure chest that can never be pirated away.

Less and More

Fear less, hope more; Eat less, chew more; Whine less, breathe more; Talk less, say more; Love more, and all good things will be yours.

— Swedish Proverb

This proverb is one of my absolute favorites, and if I followed it to a tee there isn't a doubt in my mind that I would be happier by leaps and bounds every day. The first is a biggie: fearing less. My fear is often linked to an out-of-control to-do list, one that's so long it spreads onto bits of paper that travel from desk to purse to nightstand. Its unwieldiness makes me shrink just thinking about it, and I probably spend more time fretting about the list than accomplishing anything on it.

Choose what you're going to do less of today, and reap an unexpected reward of more.

So I made a commitment to replace the fear and worry with a plan—I would do one task, or take one significant step toward completing a more complex task, every day. Just one. I immediately worried that one thing a day would never be enough, that the monster list would get even longer, but I resolved to stick with it and see what happened. I put the list in a drawer out of sight for the day and focused on the task, and it turns out that when I went back to the list before going to bed I was able to cross off five things at a time—things I had managed to do on the side, as I went, without too much concentration or effort. What a wonderful feeling!

Your Magic Number

No man's fortune can be an end worthy of his being.

— SIR FRANCIS BACON

What is your magic number? How does it feel as you work toward it?

I'm thinking of a number between one and a million. Can you guess what it is? Many of us walk around with a dollar amount in our heads—an amount that, if we had it, would make us feel prosperous, secure, and successful. It may fluctuate week to week or year to year. It may be unconscious or it may be thought out, as in the case of the comedian Jim Carrey who, before he became famous, buried his father with a check for ten million dollars as a promise to himself and a tribute to his dad.

There's nothing at all wrong with the dollar amount you have in your mind. Making plans, relishing future success, working toward a goal are all worthy and exciting endeavors. We only have to be careful of welding our whole existence to that monetary goal. We have to keep in mind that we're not on this earth to give our money a great life piling up in the bank; the money is here to help us live better. If we can keep that subtle reminder with us every time we imagine our future fortunes, the amounts we actually have and the ones we imagine we might have one day can change, but the feeling of prosperity and contentment will be the same, and that's what counts.

What Will Tomorrow Bring?

Sometimes the questions are complicated and the answers are simple.

— Dr. Seuss

"Hindsight is 20/20," goes the cliché. It often takes some distance of time or space to sort out the complexities of a difficult problem. But when we do, the whole thing shrinks, as if our minds and hearts have let go of the difficulty of the situation and found a clear, essential truth.

See the simple answers all around you.

Think of being right out of high school or college—full of passion and anticipation and probably some fear. *What will my life look like? Who will I share my experiences with? Which obstacles will I leap over and which will block my path for longer than I might hope?* Wondering what life will be may be the single most complicated question we face, and yet the answer can be nothing but simple. It will be what it will be, a sequence of events, an accumulation of hopes, relationships, hard work, and difficulties. There is no figuring out the journey beyond putting one foot in front of the other and moving forward into it, whether or not your steps are sure.

We can use Dr. Seuss's wonderful quote to remind us that the 20/20 vision we long for as we peer into the future can be accessed in the present if we just refocus on what we have, where we are now, how we feel about it, and what we can do today to build our lives. That way we can leave tomorrow for tomorrow, and yesterday to the history books, and complicated questions will lose their power to paralyze.

The Taste of Home

We all have hometown appetites. Every other person is a bundle of longing for the simplicities of good taste once enjoyed on the farm or in the hometown left behind.

— CLEMENTINE PADDLEFORD

Smell and taste your way to some wonderful memories.

Ripe red tomatoes. Fish caught this morning. Maple syrup. Corn tortillas made the old fashioned way. Smell and taste, two of our senses most strongly related to emotional memory, can carry us home in an instant. Hometown food is simple food. It's even better unadorned because it's fresh and pure. Often, the simpler the taste, the clearer the memories that flood in: Fourth of July fireworks, a night swim in summertime, or the warm ache of legs coming off the slopes and into the lodge for some hot chocolate with fresh whipped cream.

When you're going through a rough time or facing a difficult problem, one of the best remedies is to take a moment or a whole day to go back to the simple life, at least in your cooking and eating. Devote some time to simple comfort food: a bowl of chili, a cup of tea, chicken noodle soup.

Bye Bye, Extra Stuff

Order is a lovely thing; on disarray it lays its wing, teaching simplicity to sing.

— ANNA BRANCH

I recently heard a friend talking about how she had worked with someone to declutter and organize her home. The process lasted a couple of months with biweekly sessions and concentrated on helping change lifelong habits of mess and disorganization. My friend was shocked that she lost ten pounds over the course of the sessions, without even trying. She mentioned it to the organizer she'd hired and the woman laughed, "Oh, that happens all the time. I should start including it in my brochures!"

Encourage yourself to simplify, simplify, simplify and strip away what's unnecessary.

I don't know what kind of science might be behind this—are you burning extra calories heaving stacks of paper and stooping to sweep up junk? Are you replacing snack time with conscious energy aimed at cleaning and clearing out? Is it just an extension of the metaphor, that as you shed stuff you shed pounds? Is an organized kitchen or fridge a healthier one? I think most likely it's a combination of all of these, and this reminds me that we are whole beings, and what we do in one part of our life ripples into all the others.

Too Much Is Too Much

It is vain to do with more what can be done with less.

— WILLIAM OF OCCAM

Everything in proportion, whether less or more.

I went to see a play with my husband the other evening and we both came out disappointed and underwhelmed. The production was beautiful, with lavish period costumes and a lot going on. My husband summed it up by saying, "They had too much money." It seems strange to suggest that anyone in the arts might need less money, in an environment of shrinking resources all around. But what he meant was something more subtle, and more difficult to articulate: that if there had been less money there might have been more—and better—ideas about how to spend it. The thought would have had to be cleaner, clearer, and the end result would probably have been much more satisfying.

This doesn't mean that all expense is wasteful—some kinds of excessiveness can be spot on. In fashion, for example, a pair of fine, handcrafted shoes might seem excessive to some people, but the artisan who makes them has a sense of balance and the rightness of his materials and methods, and the result can be truly remarkable. In the right perspective, those shoes might be perfectly suited to a particular function, and not considered over the top in the least.

Tin Cans

It's just as unpleasant to get more than you bargain for as to get less.

— GEORGE BERNARD SHAW

Often an older generation will look at the lives of younger children and say something quaint and patronizing like: "You kids are spoiled. When I was a child all we needed was a tin can to have fun." Some of this is just a trick of memory—I'm sure that tin can could be just as boring as a video game is now, but there's also a truth there. A child who is given everything she wants immediately and without effort will soon lose the ability to motivate or regulate herself, to hold out and work toward her desires, to imagine things that are not in front of her face.

It might not be very pleasant to get less than we want or have bargained for, but getting more can be its own curse, especially if it saps us of our imagination or our drive to create more, do more, achieve more. We can take it as a blessing when our wish list is not yet fulfilled, and know that the feeling of wanting something is a wonderful and positive thing. It's far better than being apathetic as we sit in the middle of too much of everything we might ever want. That seems like its own special form of torture.

Look at a tin can and think of ten fun things to do with it, and then go back to some modern technology and enjoy that too!

23

Mum's the Word

I like people who refuse to speak until they are ready to speak.
— LILLIAN HELLMAN

If you don't have anything real to say, you needn't say anything at all.

A friend of our family had a child who was over two years old before he said much of anything. He would make some noises, and got very good at conveying his meaning without words, even to perfect strangers. He was evaluated by doctors and speech therapists, and nobody found much of anything wrong with him. His parents were beside themselves, worried that he wasn't developing normally and frustrated that no one seemed to be able to help them.

Then one morning he walked into the kitchen where his mother was doing dishes and said, "I want a piece of toast, please." Clear as day. His mother's jaw dropped to the floor and the child, a bit annoyed, repeated "toast, please!"

I don't know if he didn't speak because he wasn't physically ready, or because he felt he was being understood fine without speaking. His mother's thought, and it seems right to me, is that he is fundamentally a kind of perfectionist. That he didn't want to be caught with his tongue wagging before he knew the words would come out just right. He knew he wanted to skip baby talk altogether, so he just waited until he could.

In an age of twenty-four hour talking heads on the news and constant electronic headlines, messages, and updates, I find myself longing for people who don't say a word until they are good and ready. How refreshing.

Bit by Bit

To be satisfied with a little, is the greatest wisdom; and he that increaseth his riches, increaseth his cares; but a contented mind is a hidden treasure, and trouble findeth it not.

— AKHENATON

A close friend of my family's, a woman with whom I spent many happy afternoons when I was a child, bought a diamond ring with aluminum cans. It was not a direct exchange, of course, and it took years to accomplish. She would simply pick up discarded cans everywhere she went. This was long before it was chic—or even common—to recycle. She turned in the cans for a few cents each, and kept the money tucked away. She chose a beautiful antique ring in a store and kept it in mind as inspiration and motivation, and when she finally made enough to buy it she wore it every day, and loved telling people how she earned it. She got a real kick out of seeing their reactions.

Don't let the little stuff get you down—let it add up to something better!

Any simple action we do with a sense of purpose is multiplied through repetition. Religious teachers know this, athletes know this, even someone knitting a sweater knows this. Repetition can turn even the most mundane action, like picking up discarded cans, into something precious. Think of this the next time you're washing dishes, or writing an email, or tuning up your car. Little things can seem trivial, but put them in their greater context and we can appreciate them a bit more.

A Good Soak

I can't think of any sorrow in the world that a hot bath wouldn't help, just a little bit.

— SUSAN GLASEE

A bath might not solve all your problems, but it certainly can help a little bit.

I once knew a woman who took a hot bath every day. When I met her I was working seventy hours a week at two jobs and felt lucky if I got in a shower every other day. Soaking in a tub seemed like an impossible indulgence (and, worse than that, one that would have to be earned only by completing a half-hour session of vigorous tub scrubbing, given the state of the grout in there).

It's not that she was in some elite class—she worked hard too, but she just made taking that bath one of her priorities. I resolved to find the time to enjoy that luxury at least once a week. There is no simpler change you can make than taking the time to bathe the slow way. You don't even have to linger very long. There's just something about full submersion in piping hot water that reboots the system. After all, it's the state in which we all started life—floating, safe, and warm.

A Good Laugh

A well-developed sense of humor is the pole that adds balance to your steps as you walk the tightrope of life.

— WILLIAM ARTHUR WARD

I don't care what kind of thing makes you laugh—for my grandfather it was jokes so raunchy they'd make Howard Stern blanch. My son has been gonzo for slapstick since he was six months old. My mother loves puns, even the silliest ones. No matter what does it for us, we all could stand to fulfill our need to laugh more often. Laughing oxygenates our bloodstream, fills us with endorphins, can even change our brain chemistry. Laughter is solace, medicine, a tension diffuser.

Do your best to crack someone up today, and give in to giggling whenever possible.

Perhaps more importantly, a cultivated sense of humor is the most direct line I know to finding balance in your life. It keeps your ego in check to laugh at yourself; it lifts your spirits to let yourself be tickled even on the darkest days. Laughing with friends gives us the chance to deepen our relationships and learn new things about each other.

It's not easy navigating through the difficult moments in our lives, and there are scores of situations in which it would seem almost impossible to imagine yourself laughing. But if you're open to the possibility of finding joy in adversity, delighting in absurdity, or just plain exchanging dumb punch lines, you'll find yourself and those around you are better off and more ready to meet the challenges you all face.

Down to the Skivvies

Brevity is the soul of wit.

—WILLIAM SHAKESPEARE

Stripping away can create quite a stir.

Additionally, as Dorothy Parker quipped, "brevity is the soul of lingerie." Some things are just better smaller, shorter, tighter. But in lingerie as in witticisms, the fit matters most. It's got to make sense, be suitable in some way, in order to go the distance. Whether you're using humor to make a point or donning lace to entice and inspire, stretching the limits of propriety is best done in the spirit of less is more. Simple is good, but don't forget to leave a little something to the imagination. In either case, you probably get more out of the words or the undergarments when there's at least a bit of work to be done to expose the—ahem!—truth of the matter.

Beyond clever words and bits of ribbon and lace, we might all stand to do away with that extra bit. Try an exercise of cutting everything in half for one day. Half the calories, half the workload, half the caffeine, half the sleep (wink, wink). Then you can afford to double up on a few things: smiles and laughter, stolen moments with that special someone, time spent having a blast.

Resourcefulness

There is a treasure in being poor. It is hidden for those fortunate ones who know the values of soul treasure.

— R U M I

Bless your poverty and start getting some new ideas.

The wonderful series of children's books called *All-of-a-kind Family* by Sydney Taylor and Helen John chronicles the lives of a family living in New York City tenements in the early 20th century. The family is very poor, but resourceful, and everyone pitches in with the chores. There's one story in which the mother notices that her children aren't doing a very thorough job of dusting the front room so she announces that on dusting days there may or may not be any number of pennies hidden around the parlor. After that, the kids all jump at the chance to do the dusting, and they pore over every nook and cranny inspecting for pennies and doing an immaculate job of dusting along the way.

I am not one to glamorize poverty, but I do appreciate that, as long as our basic needs are met, there can be a wonderful ingenuity born out of a lack of resources. Children do better learning that there are huge rewards when everyone chips in (whether they pick up a penny along the way or not). Adults and children alike can recognize the true value of things and, more importantly, of people and relationships. When we live lives saturated with everything we need and the possibility of getting everything we might ever hope to need we can easily lose sight of those values.

Inheritance

A little integrity is better than any career.
— RALPH WALDO EMERSON

What are you going to leave to your children? This is a question that occupies many of us, and haunts some. Life insurance companies love to prey on this fear, that we will never have enough to leave our kids to keep them comfortable and happy when we pass on. Only a lump sum, they tell us, will suffice. And of course it's true, the death of a parent is a huge blow to a family in every way, and the financial part of it can be devastating.

Whenever you go, the biggest comfort you can leave to those around you is a life well-lived.

You could leave them with nothing. Or you could leave them with plenty of cash but poor in other respects: with no sense of integrity, or poor in their lack of wonderful memories of you. You could leave them worse off by teaching them by example that going into the consuming fear of what you can't control, or what happens beyond your death, is a worthwhile endeavor, when in fact it can suck the life right out of you. Leave them with the memory of a life lived by example and action full of love and humanity, and with the inspiration of your courage in the face of your fears.

Happiness in Small Bites

The bliss even of a moment still is bliss.

—JOANNA BAILLIE

Too often I catch myself in a thought pattern of scarcity: I don't have enough of the things I think I need, like money, time, or happiness, and I have far too much of things I'd rather do without, like stress, fear, and dust bunnies. When I do catch a breath of something wonderful it seems all too fleeting, and the relentless pull of scarcity returns. Then it gets even worse—I take that opportunity to feel even more despondent, thinking about how great it is to feel great, but how cruddy it is that I don't feel that way more often.

Even if you want more, a little bit can be plenty.

Enough already! Cake eaten in small bites is still cake, just as happiness in fits and starts is still happiness. Every time you discount a moment of bliss simply because of how quickly it comes and goes, you rob yourself of what could be a lovely experience, and drain the satisfaction that could otherwise refresh and renew you. Why bother? The next time you are happy, just enjoy. Simple enough. The next time you feel stressed, remember that five minutes of being calm or doing something you love is enough.

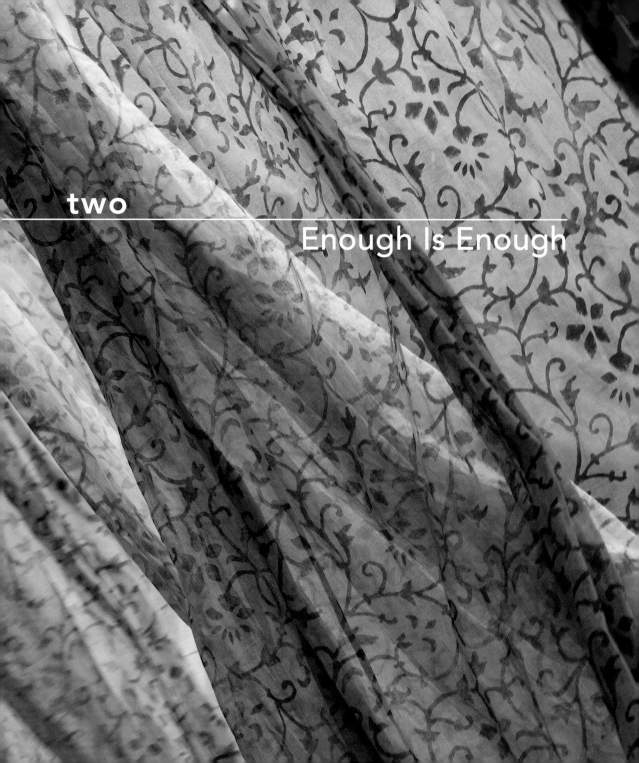

two

Enough Is Enough

Finding Balance, Making Do, and Moving Beyond

Have you heard of the Law of Plenty? This is the maxim that states that whatever we could need or want, we have already. Even if we don't literally have something plunked down in front of us, we certainly already have access to the raw materials in our lives right here and now, available and ready to be put to the task.

In order to use this rule to our advantage we have to be willing to see and understand what we have. This goes beyond taking inventory of our possessions; it is an inclusive, honest, open understanding of everything we are and have access to. To do this, we have to quit nay-saying and cut out the complaining and thinking we'll never have enough, or that we'll never amount to anything. We have to get innovative and be able to see new possibilities within the old scenarios, to understand how and when to recycle and renew our resources to get the absolute most out of them. In the process, we'll come to a wonderful balance that engenders a new, thrilling freedom. All without spending a dime.

Finding Balance

Fortunate indeed, is the man who takes exactly the right measure of himself, and holds a just balance between what he can acquire and what he can use.

— PETER MERE LATHAM

Paint a clear picture of the changing landscape of your own economy: personally, in your community, in the environment.

In hard times we become acutely aware of economy. Not only *the* economy, meaning the financial system of our world, or finding more economical ways to do things, but economy itself, which is really just another way to think about the balance created by things coming and going. Everything has its own economy—a business, a forest, a body. Materials and energy coming in, materials and energy going out.

When we are out of balance, when the coming and going are tilted too far in one direction or the other, we feel it acutely: the emptiness of a hungry stomach or the void of an overstuffed, selfish society. Balance is the key, and in order to achieve and maintain that balance we have to be honest with ourselves about what our real economic needs are.

Taking a measure of ourselves is not an easy process, but we can all stand to check in and check up on what we want, what we need, and how we can get those things. We can also look carefully at the greater economy of our community: how getting what we want, or more of what we think we need, is affecting those around us.

Wanting What You Have

Prosperity depends more on wanting what you have than
having what you want.

— GEOFFREY F. ABERT

True prosperity brings
real happiness.

Happiness is in the eye of the beholder. This is a scientific fact,
proven by many studies. Consider the anecdotal evidence:
there are happy sheep herders, and miserable ones. There are
passionate therapists and some that are burned out and done
in. For every place in society, educated or not, rich or poor,
there are people in all ranges and temperaments. There are
also those who manage to become more glum as their status
or situation gets better, or (though it's less common) to get
happier as things get worse.

Individually we tend to think that our happiness depends
on our circumstances, and only on our circumstances. It gives
us a strange kind of comfort to file through a series of events
that we may or may not be remembering in a clear way and
link them conclusively to our present state: My mother left
me, so I can't trust anyone. Or, we never had enough growing up, so I've got to hoard whatever money comes my way.
These are powerful beliefs, so much so they can create their
own realities of mistrust or financial anxiety. But we can all
learn that happiness is a matter of perspective, and when we
change our views about what prosperity really means and
how it makes us feel we might even break through to a new
kind of happiness, one in which we already have everything
we need.

Just Enough

I think knowing what you cannot do is more important than knowing what you can do. In fact, that's good taste.

— L UCILLE B ALL

Too often I find myself stretched thin to breaking. I'm overextended, overworked, and underslept. At the same time, I find that when I do stumble upon a free afternoon I don't do half of the things I think I ought to. I sit in a slump, paralyzed by a to-do list that stretches to two pages. I envy those people who can say "no" when they are asked to lead that committee or do that errand, and I desperately want a membership card to their club. I'll also happily join the group of people who get one thing done at a time and on time instead of running around trying to do it all at once, leaving the litter of half finished projects and errands everywhere they go.

I can choose not to overextend, I can choose to bite off just as much as I can chew.

Do what you can do. No more, no less. That's my new mantra.

I *can* take on projects that mean something to me, or that I want to do with someone I care about. I can also remember that when I start to make better decisions about what I can and can't do, I will probably find new reserves of time and energy to get more done. (Who knows how much time and energy is wasted on worrying alone?) I *can* get things done in small chunks—spending 20 munutes to solve part of a problem. I feel so much better using that time on something I *can* do than on sitting around moping about what I *can't*, and it's a huge relief.

Zero, Zilch, Not a Thing

It takes a lot of time to be a genius. You have to sit around so much doing nothing, really doing nothing.

—GERTRUDE STEIN

When is the last time you did a whole day of nothing? My godmother is fond of saying that there are many things that can only be accomplished by going away on vacation. By which I always think she means that we need to get out of our routine and into a new pattern to learn a new skill, or make a discovery, or fall in love. Those things often hide from us behind the repetitious familiarity of our "normal" life. Getting out of a routine can get us out of a rut, and most of us don't take nearly enough time to give nothing a chance. We even take vacations that are orderly, planned, and jam packed, and we come back more exhausted than we left.

Tell your to-do list to take a hike. Sit down. Breathe. Repeat.

Make a commitment to stoke the flame of your inner genius by doing nothing. And no cheating, either; you're not allowed to sit around feeling guilty about what you aren't getting done, because feeling guilty is a whole lot of "doing" if you ask me. You don't have to do it for a week or even a whole day at a time (though I wholeheartedly recommend a twenty-four-hour nothing binge). You can set aside an hour to do nothing. It might take some practice to calm your mind and will probably take a few sessions before you can naturally stop the flow of manic doing, but believe me, it's worth it.

Making Choices

The great thing to learn about life is, first, not to do what you don't want to do, and, second, to do what you do want to do.

— MARGARET ANDERSON

My parents' method of discipline when I was a child was based on choices. For everything they wanted me to do, they offered a choice. At bedtime I could choose to walk or be carried to the bedroom. I could pick what time I wanted to do my homework. I got to choose which vegetable I wanted to eat with dinner. And as a kid I felt very secure, and loved the sense that I was in charge of those things, never realizing once that my parents were brilliantly avoiding many of the power struggles we might otherwise have had about going to bed, finishing my homework, or eating my peas.

Make decisions. Practice every day. Get in a habit of choosing, choosing, choosing.

Feeling like we have some control over our destinies is one of life's great necessities and pleasures. Feeling like we have no choice is the fastest route to disenfranchisement and misery.

The big secret is that we always have a choice. Always. Even when it seems like we don't. We do. We can always do the thing we want to do. Yes, I'm talking about basic, everyday wants, but even more I'm talking about those deep, deep desires. We may not be able to do the thing we want to do in just the perfect way we've imagined right away tomorrow, but if you break that impulse down it's mostly about control and not about your deep original desire anyway. Get to the root of that desire and go for it. Make the choice.

The Game of Life

Resolve to take fate by the throat and shake a living
out of her.

—LOUISA MAY ALCOTT

I have a friend who just lost her job at a company she'd worked
at for five years, joining the ranks of the unemployed.
Amazingly, she was undeterred. She immediately started her
own business, doing a slightly different and more complex ver-
sion of what she'd been paid to do in the past. Business didn't
kick in immediately, and her savings winnowed. I called to offer
support and she thanked me but said she didn't need it. Six
months later she had more clients than she could take on, and
was considering hiring an employee to help out. I finally got to
ask her what had kept her going and kept her spirits up. "You
weren't even scared," I said, "you just kept on going."

"Are you kidding?" she gasped. "I was petrified."

She told me that she was so overwhelmed she stayed in
bed for a whole weekend after being laid off. She didn't know
what to do and she didn't have much time to figure it out,
and the thoughts swirling around in her head just made her
want to sleep. Then she realized it wasn't doing any good. A
competitive person and avid tennis player, she reframed the
whole thing in her head. It was going to be a game, and it
was going to be a thrill to come out on top. Every challenge
she met, she felt free to improvise and be imaginative because
she had thoroughly convinced herself that the stakes were not
life or death, but just a game.

*Make your stakes whatever
you need them to be to
grab hold of your problem
by the collar.*

Balancing Act

The truth is balance. However, the opposite of truth, which is unbalance, may not be a lie.

— SUSAN SONTAG

Sometimes I catch myself turning positive thinking inside out. That is, I'm struggling to make everything in my life add up to a sort of wonderful equation, where everything is balanced and comes out brilliantly in the end. I think there really must be a way to get to this place, and my wheels start to grind in the process. If I'm having a bad day, I try to force myself to think or experience something positive, and by pushing it I end up far worse off than I started.

It's okay to be off-kilter. In fact, it may be bringing you closer to the balance you seek.

When we come to a truthful understanding of a problem or a challenge, we are often surprised by the simple balance of the solution. We usually come to that understanding by a route that is unsought, or at least unfamiliar to us. The balance is a surprise, a gift.

When we're stuck in a state of unbalance, negativity, or fear, we can't get out of it by pretending to look for balance, or by forcing ourselves to find some kind of middle ground. We can only submit to the truthfulness of the imbalance and do our best to tune into new ways to see a clearer, simpler picture.

Peaceful Practice

He who sweats more in peace, bleeds less in war.

— P R O V E R B

Spending our energy on building peace can save us the cost of war.

This proverb can be read a couple of different ways. Does it say that he who toils harder at building weapons of war during peacetime will come out on top when a conflict actually arises? Maybe, though I think a better reading is in the importance of working diligently at the task of peace: the negotiating, building alliances, gathering information and striving toward peace and justice for all. When we put our hand to those things during peacetime we can look forward to less bloodshed during wartime or, even better, no wars at all.

The dream of an end to all war can seem illusive at best, impossible at worst. In anticipation of coming wars we stay prepared, throwing a lot of funding and manpower behind those preparations. What if we diverted a little bit at a time to preparations for peace? And then a little more? And a little more? What if we took the hard work of peace as seriously as the tasks of war?

Clear Signals

The more elaborate our means of communication,
the less we communicate.

—JOSEPH PRIESTLEY

The paradox of communi-
cation tells us that saying
less can mean more.

In his comment Joseph Priestley has clear insight into our over-taxed communication culture. Saturated with cell phones, texting, emailing, and the internet, we seem to chatter more and more and say (and hear) less and less. Funny that he was able to glean such incisive perspective on our modern condition even though he passed away in 1804. Yes, that's not a typo. Priestley was a chemist and clergyman who died in 1804, more than 200 years ago.

Apparently, even then, it was clear to some people that in order to really say something, we don't need much in the way of elaborate stuff—whether it's flowery language or expensive doohickeys. The more we say, and the more complex our means of saying it, the more diluted our message and the feelings behind it can become.

When it comes to expressing ourselves, less is almost always more. Telling a story without adornment, dealing plainly in business transactions, stripping away our emotional baggage to deal more directly with our loved ones, all of these are simple ways to make our day-to-day lives feel more full and more connected.

Common Ground

For parlor use, the vague generality is a life saver.

— GEORGE ADE

It is an underappreciated blessing to be a part of a social circle that includes people who have wildly different viewpoints
and ideologies. I just learned that Supreme Court justices
Ruth Bader Ginsburg and Antonin Scalia, the members of the
court considered to embody the farthest opposing ideologies,
are the closest personal friends among those who serve on
the court. While I can't imagine they only speak in generali-
ties, I have a feeling that there are certain subjects that don't
bear too much back and forth, and moments in which less is
more rules the day.

*There is no harm in find-
ing common ground and
traveling it together.*

Civil society can be a kind of tightrope, especially when
you're dealing with cranky in-laws, bosses' spouses, and the
like. There are some who seem truly at ease on that particular
tightrope, and I think it's because they trust that you don't
have to go into a whole lot of detail about your personal life
or your political convictions to have a good time. In fact,
given half a chance and a touch of decorum, you might actually enjoy that blessing of decidedly mixed company.

Don't Sweat the Small Stuff

Men often bear little grievances with less courage than they do large misfortunes.

— A E S O P

You can face any difficulty with poise and calm.

You're halfway through the ten-person line at the grocery store, and you're about to scream. The toddler in front of you has already smeared chocolate on your winter coat, the ice cream for your dinner party is melting, and the person at the head of the line is embarking on a long paragraph of haggling about a sale price and a rain check. We all get testy in these everyday situations, and it's perfectly understandable. Why is it though that when we're truly in a moment of danger or adversity, when one would argue we really have something to make a fuss about, we most often have the opposite reaction?

In the middle of a tragedy we often don't have time to take stock, and we know that we may need every bit of emotional and mental energy we have to keep ourselves safe, so we don't waste any on petty grievances or major outbursts.

When we let ourselves get really frustrated about little things, whether or not we're justified in doing so, we allow those things to sap our resources. It's tricky, because when we're not facing that life or death moment we don't give it a second thought to get bent out of shape. But if possible we should try to meet the small challenges in the same spirit we might for something a bit heavier—getting too worked up might do us harm in the long run.

Life's Work

A stitch in time saves nine.

— P R O V E R B

Preparation, meditation, inspiration. Make maintenance your life's work.

My grandma used to say that life is ninety percent maintenance. When she said that I'd try to smile and nod, but my heart would sink. I found it so depressing, almost dehumanizing, to think that all there was to life was regular upkeep. As if brushing your teeth after meals and vacuuming the parlor once a week were the sum total of our existence.

Like all grandmotherly sayings, though, this one has a deeper meaning. Yes, cleaning and mending and stocking the fridge are all maintenance and, yes, those things all must be done with some kind of regularity for the rest of our lives. So the first part of the message is "get over it!" If those things are ninety percent of life, why waste time getting in a tizzy over them? Faster and easier to do them now and save time and energy than to wait until things get out of hand.

The second message is my grandmother's broad definition of what maintenance is. In her mind, maintenance was really anything worth doing, and it was her way of finding meaning in all things. For example, reading maintains your mental acuity, spending time with friends and family maintains the connections that help you enjoy the good times and weather the bad ones. Exercise maintains your body. Enjoying art maintains your soul. When I look at it this way, I start to hope for a life that is one hundred percent devoted to maintenance.

Take Half

Simplicity is making the journey of this life with just baggage enough.

— CHARLES DUDLEY WARNER

Jettison the extra stuff and find the power of simplicity.

I have a rule of thumb my mother taught me about packing for a long trip: lay out everything you think you need, and then take half the stuff and twice the money. I've found that even the times I don't have twice as much money to bring along, I can still take half of what I think I need and never miss the rest of it.

If this rule of thumb were adapted into a life lesson, you might say that when setting out on any new adventure—whether it's a new job, a move, or going back to school—you should take half the stuff you're holding onto. That could be "stuff" in the form of old habits, ideas, or hang ups. Or it could be literal stuff, as in draw a line down the middle of your garage and pick what's going with you and what's going to be donated to people who need it. Then, instead of taking twice as much money, take twice as much energy and inspiration. Do whatever it takes to boost your drive to go after your new purpose, your new direction, your new goal. Elevate the level of intensity for going after what you want to twice what you think you need, and with all that extra baggage gone, you'll be surprised at how fast you get there.

Renewable Resources

Old places and old persons in their turn, when spirit
dwells in them, have an intrinsic vitality of youth which
is incapable, precisely, the balance and wisdom that
come from long perspectives and broad foundations.

— GEORGE SANTAYANA

In the past couple of years it's thankfully become trendy to reduce, reuse, and recycle. Old barns become new furniture; used metal, glass and plastic make their way into modern industry, and we have everything from green household linens to green computers. In some ways we haven't quite made the next logical leap though, that the old places and persons among us, in their turn, are not expendable or disposable, but instead carry within them a spirit that is forever young and new. Most cultures have an intrinsic reverence for their elders, something that in our society is either utterly forgotten or feels at best like a quaint nicety. But just as recycling may save our planet, truly honoring the spirit of who and what has come before might just have the power to save our humanity.

We desperately need those long perspectives and broad foundations.

By all means we should look to coming generations to solve the many problems that face us, and we should also tap into the vast resources of existing generations as they age. Our vitality need not be correlated to the age of our bodies and minds, and our growth as a society cannot be sustainable without honoring what has come before.

Old Friends

Prosperity is no just scale; adversity is the only balance
to weigh friends.

— P L U T A R C H

*Keeping your friends in
balance is one of life's
great rewards.*

It's easy to make new friends and keep our friendships strong
when things are going well and we feel good about ourselves.
We're more fun to be around, we're happier, and we don't tax
our friendships with any minor hardships.

When things take a turn for the worse, we can learn very
quickly who our truest friends are. But that's not a bad thing.
I'd much rather have the love and support of a couple of close
pals during hard times than a general wash of useless sym-
pathy from everyone I know. And I'll gladly step up for those
same close friends whenever they need me, but I know my
limits and I can't afford to do that for every acquaintance.

The important thing is to balance my close friendships in
good times and bad, to provide a counterweight of happiness
and prosperity for those who are down, and never to be
afraid to ask for the same if I find myself down in the dumps.
That is, after all, what friends are for.

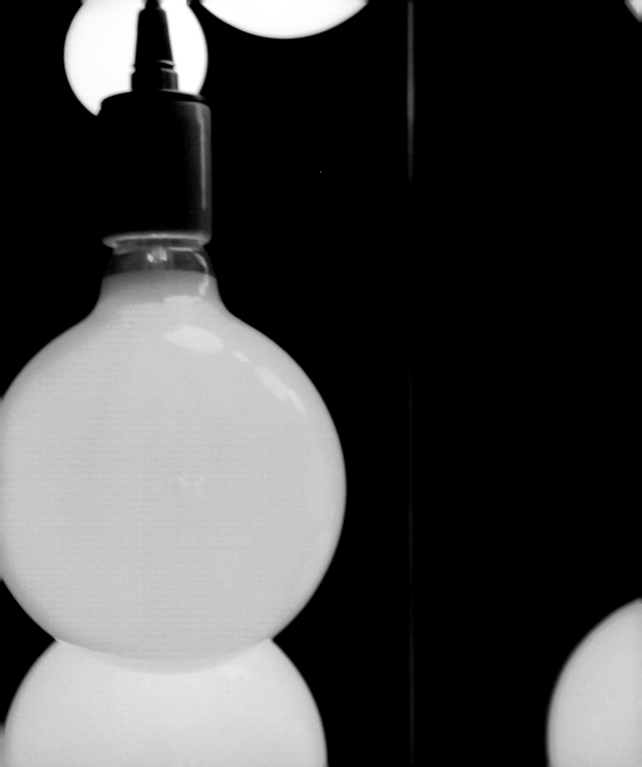

Cunning and Creativity

In art and dream may you proceed with abandon. In life
may you proceed with balance and stealth.

— PATTI SMITH

Difficult challenges call for creative solutions. Being creative
can be scary. Making something out of nothing can feel
impossible. You have to go out on a limb and really let yourself go in order to even get started. Sometimes I shut down
my own creative impulses with a convenient excuse: being a
creative dreamer is fine, but when it comes to real life I'd better buckle down and get serious.

*Dreamy inspiration and
shrewd intellect are just
about the perfect com-
plements to each other.*

We don't have to be insane artistic types to find creative
solutions to things. A little compartmentalizing can be help-
ful; let yourself go whole hog into the world of dreams, aspi-
rations, inspirations, and at the same time, allow yourself to
apply those dreams in purposeful, direct, or even cunning
ways in "real life." The trick, as with so many things, is in the
balance of the two. Slide too far one way and you get lost in
the clouds, losing your drive to get through ordinary life;
swing back the other way and find yourself pushing hard to
make uninspired ideas work to your advantage.

Love, Love, Love

Love is a verb.

— CLARE BOOTHE LUCE

Love more, and then some more, and then some more on top of that.

Love is a verb and, to quote The Beatles, love is all you need. When we have enough love, we have enough of everything else. And the commodity of love has its own wonderful rules: it can't be diminished by giving it away; it provides a high return of investment; it increases exponentially when shared freely.

When we love, we create. When we love, we work hard. When we love, we appreciate. When we love, we grant freedom. When we love, we understand. When we love, we renew that which we love and we rejuvenate ourselves.

An active verb, loving must be done and redone, over and over, day after day and year after year. There is no finish line and no high-water mark for loving. This can feel daunting in those inevitable moments when it's hard to flow love to something that doesn't seem to deserve it, or to someone who's making us miserable. But even those moments are part of the blessing of love—loving can transform the thing we love, and it can transform our own hearts. Love is never wasted, and can never be undone. Loving more than you ever thought possible will open the door to even more loving. What a gift.

three
What You See Is What You Get

Outlook, Attitude, and Optimism

Changing your life might be as easy as changing your outlook. Or, if you're more inclined to a glass half empty view of things, you might say that changing your life might be as hard as changing your outlook. How we see the world makes us who we are, and ultimately our attitude defines and informs our feelings and our circumstances.

"What you see is what you get" is a reminder that our outlook defines our existence. It also helps us remember that things may be as simple as they seem, and we don't need to benefit by making a commitment to seeing and evaluating things truthfully, whenever and however we possibly can. We must also never forget that no matter how bad things get, optimism is always an option. And usually the best one.

Magic Mirror

We don't see things as they are. We see them as we are.

— ANAÏS NIN

What if you had a magical mirror, one that could truly give you a picture of how everyone else sees you? What would surprise you? What would delight you? What would you undertake to change about yourself, if anything?

We may never have a magical mirror, unless we find it in other people's perspectives.

"Mirror, mirror, on the wall. . . who's the fairest of them all?" intones the wicked queen in Snow White. She is shocked when for the first time, the mirror tells her she's not the fairest. We all know what happens next. But I'm wondering if that mirror might have stayed with its old line if the queen had continued to believe that she was, in fact, the most beautiful. After all, there is no objective standard of beauty; nobody agrees on the one most perfect face. So maybe that queen was just seeing her own fear reflected back at her, her terror of becoming older, less attractive.

We see ourselves, and the world around us, through our own eyes. For all our attempts at objectivity, it can never be any other way. And while this might feel like a limitation, it really isn't. It's a gift because it requires us to step out of the isolation of ourselves. The closest we can ever get to seeing things for what they really are is through communication and understanding, coming outside of our own palace walls and doing our best to puzzle through the experiences, preferences, and viewpoints of those around us.

Getting Up Again

What we call failure is not the falling down, but the staying down.

— MARY PICKFORD

When I was a teenager I read a horoscope that claimed that people born under the alignment of stars I was born under would generally do quite well in life, enjoying excellent health and stamina and able to successfully achieve their desired goals. But it warned that failure would make us "drop like flies." I still remember the phrase, it had such an impact on me; it tapped into a part of my character I'd rather let go. I have always been terrified of failure, and have often relied on that terror as a motivating force to get things done, be thought well of, and force myself out of a slump. In indulging that fear of failure, I have managed to almost completely shut out and shut down the only thing that can save me from the inevitable failures I face in my life: the ability to pick myself up and move on.

Reclaim the privilege of falling and failing, and learn to get up again.

Fear as a motivator can only take me so far. Fear can't hold a candle to inspiration. Fear elevates failure to the status of the grim reaper—always waiting, ready to cut me down and wrench me from my life and loved ones. But when I'm inspired, passionately going after something, failure can never have that kind of power. Instead, it becomes a stepping stone, a lesson learned, a warning, or even a new opportunity in disguise.

Making Meaning

The word *happiness* would lose its meaning if it were not balanced by sadness.

— CARL JUNG

The more we accept and appreciate one extreme, the more likely we are to be able to feel the depth of the opposite extreme.

If you ate caviar every day for lunch it would probably start to taste like canned tuna. If we all wore tuxedos and ball gowns to work every day we'd forget to notice how beautiful they are. If we were on a perpetual vacation and not allowed to work or do anything to better ourselves, we would surely go mad. It's just the same with our emotions. We romanticize the idea of being happy all the time, but happiness itself could be reduced to a kind of dull boredom if it weren't for the shades of feeling within and around it. Where would we be without heartbreak, longing, and anger, let alone agitation, passion, adventure?

Things are defined as much for what they are as for what they are not. We know that a spoon is a spoon because of its spooniness but also because it is different in some very basic ways from a fork. Every cloud has a silver lining, and every silver living has a cloud. We couldn't see one if it weren't for the other. Our job is to appreciate the opposites and remember that we get the most out of life in the dynamic pull between them: happiness and misery, love and hate, hard work and leisure.

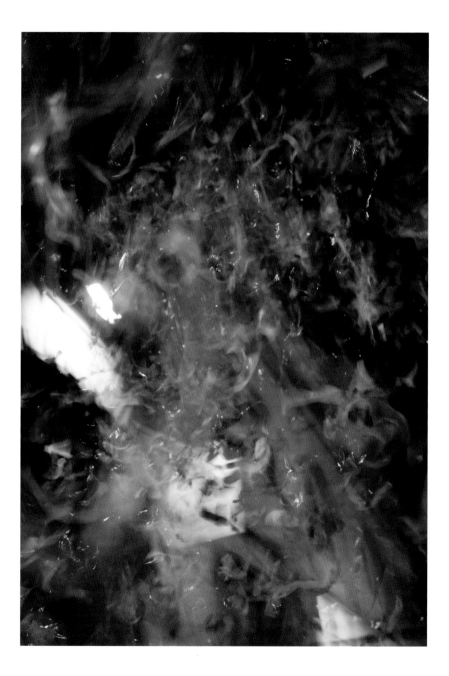

People Pleasing

The more one pleases everybody, the less one pleases profoundly.

— STENDHAL

You can't please everyone all of the time, so work on your own happiness and that of the people you love the most.

I can't make everybody happy. It's not for lack of trying, believe me. I'll try until I'm blue in the face: listening, responding, trying new things, smoothing over differences, hoping everybody likes me, wanting everyone to have a good time. At the end of a day of people pleasing I drop into bed, exhausted.

Making everyone around you happier by trying to please them all at once is an insidious little trap. It sounds wonderful, and it might be, if it were possible. More importantly, the impulse to please leads us down roads that are not known for inspiring true, deep happiness and affection in anyone. Our desire to please usually comes from a fear of not being liked. As we work to please we placate, we compromise, and we stifle our own and others' feelings toward some perceived greater good. How could any of that lead to profound pleasure?

We're better off remembering that we make people happy first by being happy ourselves, because joy spreads faster than a flu bug in winter. Second, we can only hope to inspire happiness in others by allowing room for our differences, even if they might occasionally flare up into disagreements. Third, we make people happy by paying attention and learning about what excites and inspires them, and figuring out special ways to nurture those feelings in a way that brings us delight at the same time.

Tune Up

Let other pens dwell on guilt and misery.

— JANE AUSTEN

There will always be plenty of whining to go around. Plenty of angry bitterness. Plenty of guilt trips and more than enough nagging and wheedling. Why bother to add your voice to that negative chorus?

I sometimes catch myself thinking that I have to complain. If I don't, who will? Granted, standing up for injustice, or working to change peoples' lives for the better—those things may require a bit of loudmouthed complaining, but they need even more loving action to really be on their way to genuine improvement. The complaining that we all do everyday about things that are beyond our control or might as well be (like the weather and the stock market), let's choose to leave that particular melody to someone else, at least for today. Then maybe tomorrow it'll be easier not to join in and sing along, and the day after that maybe we'll start up our own tune of gratitude, or inspiration, or determination.

Sing it out, march to your own drummer, and dance to a different, more positive beat.

Simplicity at Last

Simplicity is the final achievement. After one has played a vast quantity of notes and more notes, it is simplicity that emerges as the crowning reward of art.

— FREDERIC CHOPIN

Enjoy each stepping stone on your way to that reward of simplicity.

It seems that truly great artists often make a complete circle in their lives from an initial spark of creative genius into a long period spent perfecting every detail of their art, and finally coming back around to something that more closely resembles that first spark, but is only what is most simple, essential and graceful. Pablo Picasso described the process by saying, "It took me four years to paint like Raphael, but a lifetime to paint like a child."

Simplicity exists at the starting and ending point of any great learning process, whether it's artistic, spiritual, or scientific. Many of us never stay the course to enjoy that final turnaround to wonderful simplicity—we think we aren't talented enough, or we burn out when things get too complicated or seem to be taking too long. But the simple repetition of notes and more notes or brushstroke after brushstroke will yield far more than the sum of its parts. The act of thoughtful repetition bears itself out in the most satisfying reward imaginable. A return to childlike simplicity in a whole new dimension of skill and freedom. Whether it's in our careers, our parenting, at church, or in the studio, this is surely a wonderful pursuit.

Multiplication Tables

Perpetual optimism is a force multiplier.

— COLIN POWELL

Time to supersize your next project with a major dose of optimism.

Say you're looking at a problem at work or at home. You have a team in the form of the people around you, you have certain resources at your disposal including raw materials, money, and the special talents of your team. If you manage to get together and organize and strategize you might just come up with a good solution: a new pitch for that account at work, or a renovated basement done with your own hands.

Any team should look for a force multiplier, that thing that can exponentially increase the effectiveness of a tool or a group. Pizza delivery at the right moment can be a force multiplier—it means everybody gets back to work happier. A conference call setup can be a force multiplier—get everybody off the stunted back and forth of email and really talking in a rapid-fire brainstorm.

The prime force multiplier in any group or individual is perpetual optimism. Get your hands on a bit of this and it transforms every tool at your disposal into a super helper. It elevates any idea to a moment of inspiration. Optimism is a morale booster, a salve in difficult times, a motivating force, and a pretty wonderful way to go through this life.

What Must Be Done

I have learned over the years that when one's mind is made up, this diminishes fear; knowing what must be done does away with fear.

— ROSA PARKS

The ancient Greek play *Antigone* tells the story of a young woman, Antigone, who decides she must bury her deceased brother in defiance of her uncle, the king. Her sister Ismene tries to stop her, knowing that the punishment for her actions will be certain death. At one point the sister pleads, saying that she could never be strong enough to suffer the fate that surely awaits Antigone. And Antigone responds that she's not strong either, but it doesn't matter. She knows what must be done.

Knock fear out of your way with a bit of determination.

Making up your mind solidifies the integrity of your purpose. After your mind is made up, the preoccupying questions of, Is this right? What should I do? and What will they do to me? all fall away. This is why making up your mind can feel like such a terrifying prospect. We often want to cuddle up to those difficult questions because they protect us from jumping into a complex or painful task. Making that leap becomes immeasurably easier when we remember that fear takes a hike at the first sign of that integrity of purpose. It may still be there but it will be so far in the background that it will have to release its paralyzing hold, and we will be free to do what we know we must do, regardless of what comes next.

The End of Your Rope

A little more persistence, a little more effort, and what seemed hopeless failure may turn to glorious success.

—ELBERT HUBBARD

How many stories are there in the history books in which the tide changed at the last possible moment? Defeat, demise, surrender were just around the corner and suddenly everything changed? I don't think it's false hope to believe that things can change—and change radically—at any time. I know it isn't crazy to believe in the impossible. I've seen the impossible come to pass too many times in my life and others' lives to think otherwise.

Wonderful success often waits on the very brink of failure.

When you are at the end of your rope, there is no better time to hold on with everything you've got. When you feel like giving up on a long-held dream that just isn't happening, you may be facing the final hurdle that stands in your way. There's no better time to jump. Glorious success is only attained by those who are willing to push themselves to their own limits, and beyond. That kind of success demands risk, and thrives on difficulty. So if you feel yourself in the throes of hard times and can muster the drive to keep going, to find a new approach to an old problem, to challenge yourself to rediscover the passionate impulse that got you this far, you're most likely on your way toward that glorious success.

The Life of Things

Gammy used to say, "Too much scrubbing takes the life right out of things."

— BETTY MACDONALD

Your "to feel" list ought to take precedence over that boring, lifeless, to-do list any day.

Think of how beautiful things can be with a bit more life in them—the silver candlesticks sitting on my dining room table right now are a tad tarnished, with the wax from a dinner party still clinging to them, and looking at them brings back memories of late night talking and laughing with best friends.

Housework is overrated. Or better, a minimum of housework is a lovely thing, and a maximum amount can be downright oppressive. There's a happy medium somewhere between the unpleasantness of growing unknown flora in the shower and taking away the essence of a lived-in space by cleaning it to the point of sterilization. It's a matter of priorities and perspective—do you keep better track of where dust mites might pop up than you do of your teenager's whereabouts? Have you forgotten the little things, like how to make your kids or your partner laugh harder than anything? Are you letting your to-do list get the better of that other list you should be keeping, your "to feel" list? Your "to feel" list has more fun stuff on it I bet—things like feeling exhilarated, passionate, surprised, energized.

Speed Limit

More haste, less speed.

— PROVERB

Ever have one of those days where you do everything twice? You go to the post office and wait in line, only to find when you get to the window that you've forgotten the most important thing you were meant to bring. So you have to come back. Or you type an email response to a group of people before reading through everyone else's responses and create a misunderstanding that has to be corrected with three more emails. I've even done a whole load of laundry just to make sure I had one particular shirt ready for an interview the next day, only to find the fool thing sitting at the bottom of the dirty clothes hamper, unwashed.

Not everything can (or should) be done at breakneck speed.

Our modern lives are so busy and jam-packed that we feel like we can't possibly keep up unless we're going at it full tilt all day long. We're doing more and getting less out of it all, and we try to rebalance the equation by doing even more at an ever more frantic pace, with understandably dreary outcomes. If we can remember to make ourselves do it, slowing down will at the very least help us refocus our energy and prepare for what's coming at us, and at most it will shave hours off the time we spend trying to get things done every day.

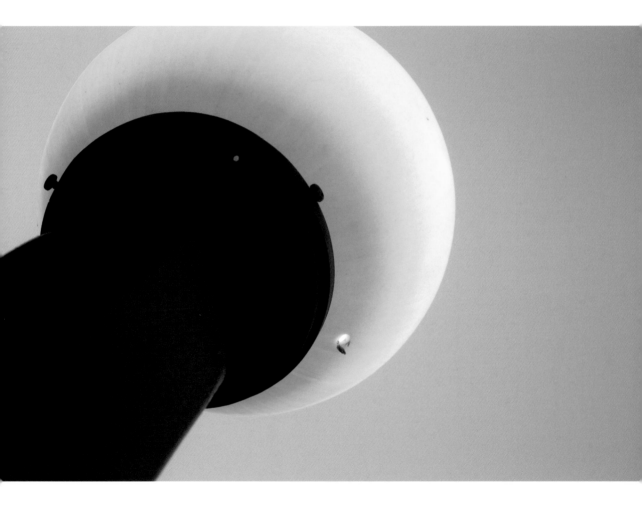

Move It!

Life is like riding a bicycle. To keep your balance you must keep moving.

— ALBERT EINSTEIN

My mother called me the other day in a funk. She was getting over a bad cold, worried about some friends who were having a hard time, fretting about finances and work and health problems. And you know what I did? I told her to go take a hike. Well, in truth I said "Why don't you go for a walk?" which sounds a bit better.

She didn't. She called me the next day though as she was walking around running errands and said, "You were right. I should have done this yesterday. I feel so much better."

It's so easy to forget the simple difference in perspective we get when we get outside. It doesn't matter if we're walking to the corner store, or running on a path near the beach, or just doing a bit of gardening in the backyard. Life looks better when we get off the couch, when we leave our desk to eat lunch, when we can see the horizon and sniff the breeze.

On the bicycle of life, when we stop moving we tip over. This goes for literally moving, like getting out of the house or office or going for a vacation and a change of scenery. It also, of course, goes for metaphorical moving—learning new things, making progress on lifelong goals, reevaluating long held beliefs.

Keep your feet on the pedals and turn, turn, turn.

Turning Off the Doubt

The more you reason the less you create.

— RAYMOND CHANDLER

Ever talk yourself out of a really good idea? I do it all the time. That first spark of something new feels great, and pretty soon I get to the leading question, "Why have I never thought of this before?"

Turn off the noise of your reasoning mind (and mouth) long enough to listen to a bit of inspiration.

Then it begins, a torrent of reasons I didn't have this idea earlier: because it isn't feasible, or it's just plain silly, or everyone will think I've lost my mind. Instantaneous idea-killers; another one bites the dust.

Now I know my habit, at least a little bit, so I've made myself a kind of muzzle. If I have a great new idea, say for a new book project, I slap a mental hand over my mouth. I'm not allowed to talk to anyone about the details, even say them out loud. Instead, I build an inner dialogue about my idea, never wondering why I hadn't thought of it before. I treat my new idea as though I've been planning it my whole life, at least until I can get my wheels turning and start to work it out.

Some ideas do turn out to be duds, no doubt about it. The secret is that exploring the dumb ideas in a spirit of openness and creativity more often than not leads straight to a really great idea that couldn't otherwise be found.

Seeking Out the Sun

The flower that follows the sun does so even on
cloudy days.

— ROBERT LEIGHTON

One thing I love about embracing the philosophy of less is
more is that it helps me do away with my all-or-nothing attitude. So often I find myself in a negative, judgmental place. If
I'm not happy, I figure I might as well be depressed. If things
aren't going my way, then they probably never will. If I can't
solve that problem or meet that goal in the next twenty-four
hours I might as well throw in the towel forever. I hardly ever
dare to speak aloud this disastrous tape-loop that runs in my
head over and over. If I did, maybe I could finally hear the
absurdity of these statements and let them fly away into the
ether once and for all.

*You too can follow the
sun behind the clouds.*

The wisdom of less is more helps us realize that sometimes getting halfway there is just enough for today. Less is
more reminds us that we don't have to do everything, feel
everything, or be at our best every day to be living the life we
want to lead. The seeds for our happiness need glowing sun-
shine and dreary grey clouds to sprout and grow into the
flowers we hope for. We need never lose sight of the more just
because we have a little less. And we can always stand to
remember that a closer look at our "less" may reveal a deeper
"more."

Great Mysteries

"The more unintelligent a man is, the less mysterious existence seems to him."

— A R T H U R   S C H O P E N H A U E R

Looking for answers, we find more questions. Oh, wonderful mystery!

At around the age of three a child starts to ask "why?" Why is the sky blue? Why are you my mommy? Why does a cow say moo? The constant questioning can drive any parent to the brink of collapse, but most parents are saved by the love they have for their kids, and by a respect for one of the most basic instincts we have as human beings: the urge toward discovery and self-discovery. It is a natural state to be curious about life and death, to wonder how things work and to try to find answers no matter how many more questions they may call up.

For whatever reason, in our education and maturation, we sometimes lose a good chunk of this innate curiosity. It is comforting to think we might actually know something about existence and our own place in it, so we come to a few conclusions and leave it at that. Only the truly genius (and often slightly mad) among us are willing to take the risk of continually embracing questions whose answers become more and more difficult as you attempt to parse them.

Listening and Responding

Why did God give me two ears and one mouth? So that I
will hear more and talk less.

— LEO ROSTEN

*Most of us could stand to
cut down by half what we
say in conversation, and
increase our listening
twofold.*

In a social situation I sometimes catch myself pretending to
listen, rehearsing the next thing I'm going to say. I'm embar-
rassed when I realize I'm doing it and I do it more than I'd
like to admit. I don't know if it's social anxiety or narcissism
or laziness or what, but either way it's an insulting and useless habit.

It's very rare to find someone who's truly a good listen-
er. It takes a lot of energy to turn down the volume of our
own inner dialogue and really hear someone else, especially
if that person is rehearsing their usual litany of complaints.
You can train yourself to listen better, even giving yourself a
little mental pop quiz after a conversation. I even just read
about a study that proved that performing a simple unrelated
task, like doodling or doing the dishes, might actually increase
our capacity to listen and retain what we're hearing. That
should come in handy next time my sister calls to complain.

It helps me too to remember that while I listen to someone's problems, I don't have to launch into a brainstorm
about how to solve those problems. The act of listening, in
and of itself, is a powerful problem solver. Just letting someone air out can often help them to get over and move past
whatever it is that's bugging them or dragging them down.

Courageous Optimism

I'm a pessimist because of intelligence, but an optimist because of will.

— A N T O N I O G R A M S C I

You may have noticed that any pessimist can back up what he says with unassailable logic. Listen long enough and you'll start to wonder why you ever thought the world was anything but a miserable pile of garbage, sinking deeper into filth every day. You'll even have some facts and figures to back up this world view. You'll be making all sorts of connections between terrible coincidences and awful statistics, and you'll probably start to feel a little queasy.

Pessimism may be our daily habit, but optimism must be our life's work.

Never forget that a pessimist lives in a kind of self-made prison. A pessimist cannot *do*, *make*, or *create* anything, because they have built a fortress around themselves that is strong and surprisingly high-maintenance—they have to work to reinforce their negativity all day long, every day. It takes a lot of effort, and there isn't much time for anything else.

It may take even more work, and will certainly take more courage, to be an optimist. Optimism so often runs counter to our intellectual assessment of things, what we think of as the truth. Only an optimist can see beyond the facts and figures, see with an inner being that it smarter than the brain. Only an optimist can make the leap of faith that it takes to chart a new course, make a new discovery, change the world in a way that no one has ever imagined.

four

Credit Where Credit Is Due

Blessings, Bonuses, and Gratitude

Embracing a philosophy of less is more has the power to flood our lives with more of what we want and need almost immediately. We can experience an immediate change without doing anything other than getting ready to see the abundance as it comes into and passes through our lives, touching everything we have and everyone we know. Blessings abound when we are open to them. Some appear out in the open as bright blossoms, and some would prefer to stay underground, quietly toiling in the soil and fertilizing our new growth.

The most important task we have in our lives is to give thanks: the simplest, purest thanks we can intone. This cannot be said enough. Gratitude, practiced early and often, can transform things through pure thought. Small things into big ones. Simple pleasures into wonderful luxuries. Grey days into nourishing rainstorms. Daily habits into devotional practice. Try it on for size; I think it'll suit you.

Simple Luxuries

Too much of a good thing is wonderful.

— M A E   W E S T

Abundance is a wonderful word and an even more wonderful thing. There are many things that are best enjoyed in profusion: simple delights like clean air and water, open vistas, fresh vegetables, and of course we can't forget sex and chocolate.

I'm a firm believer in simplifying your life and paring away whatever you don't want or need. And I'm all for filling up whatever space is freed up with the best of what you do want and need, and tons of it. You don't have to be barebones just for the sake of it, especially when it's so much fun to indulge in the things that really make you happy, whatever they may be.

Some of my favorite things are simple luxuries, things that are heavy on the extravagance but easy on the wallet: really good bath salts, homemade desserts, nice writing pens, days spent wandering through a museum. A little creativity goes a long way, and with some thought and preparation you can be indulging to the hilt with no guilt.

Sometimes less is more, but then again sometimes more is more.

Sweetness

Reflect upon your present blessings of which every man
has many—not on your past misfortunes, of which all
men have some.

— CHARLES DICKENS

Life is sweet. But it certainly doesn't strike us that way all the
time. Especially when we're stuck in a traffic jam, or slogging
through a Monday morning, or battling a bad flu. Why do we
grant so much more value to our past misfortunes than to our
present blessings? Why do we let a long line at the bank can-
cel out the memory of a wonderful morning spent with our
kids? Maybe we're just after immediate gratification, so whatever's in front of us right this moment is the prevailing feeling? I don't know, but in my own life I sure could stand to
put a little less focus on the downers and funnel a bit more
energy into the many, many things I have to be grateful for
right this moment.

*Ferret out the sweetness
in your life early and
often.*

When I get down in the dumps about any number of
things that are wrong with my present situation I make
myself sit down with a scrap of paper and a pencil. Nothing
fancy, it just needs to happen right away. I start writing, as fast
as I can, my thank you list. Things I'm truly thankful for,
things I'd like to be more thankful for. People I've never taken
the time to thank for this or that, or for just being themselves
and being a part of my life. Within a few minutes the scales are
readjusted and my mood invariably lightens. I can go back to
any daily un-pleasantries with a renewed sense of gratitude.

Owning

Learn to get in touch with the silence within yourself, and know that everything in life has purpose. There are no mistakes, no coincidences, all events are blessings given to us to learn from.

— Elisabeth Kubler-Ross

Okay, I'll admit it. I am a control freak. It's one of those things about myself I'd love to do away with completely, and yet I hang on. I'm somehow married to the faulty logic that if I can only get things going my way, if I can predict the outcomes and plan for the results, then I will live a life free of mistakes, wrongs, even free of tragedy. The further I delve into my state of controlling denial, the harder I get slammed when something unexpected or unwanted does make an appearance, which of course it inevitably does.

I own my fear. I own my mistakes. I own my forgiveness. I own my lessons and my blessings.

The biggest gift I can give myself is a daily remembrance that there are no mistakes. Nothing in this world is wrong, or bad, or unfair. Nothing that can happen to me can make me a victim, I'm the only one who has the power to do that.

Now, suffering is real. People make errors in judgment. Wrongs are committed in all kids of ways. Most of what other people do is not within my control, so I can and should lay off the gas pedal with the control stuff. The only things I can allow myself to control are how I look at those things and how I choose to respond to them. Even then, replacing the word "control" with "own" might do me a world of good. I can own my responses to negative events.

Toasty Warm

When you are grateful fear disappears and abundance
appears.

— ANTHONY ROBBINS

*What are you feeling
more because of your
fear? Can you feel an
abundance of more or
just the opposite?*

As a child I was fearless about the cold. I could go outside in
a short sleeved shirt in a Minnesota winter (much to my
mother's chagrin). I swam in frigid Lake Superior at the age
of eight. Everyone always commented that my hands and feet
were ice cold, but it never bothered me. In fact, I'm sure it
happened, but I have no memories of feeling cold until I was
a teenager. At that point I became a complete cold wimp. Icy
wind was painful and I had to bundle up every inch of my
body.

Strangely, after more than ten years, this past winter is the
first where my body seems to have re-habituated to loving the
cold. I don't know if it was conscious or something on a
chemical level. I did decide at some point during the fall that
I was sick of being cold, so I was going to do my best not to
let it bother me. I figured that some of the pain I was experi-
encing was just as much about the accumulating fear and tension as the mercury dropped as it was about actually feeling
the cold.

I don't know if it's mind over matter or not, but I don't
worry about the cold anymore. I feel warm when the temp
drops below zero, and I love going for long walks on days that
would've seen me cowering inside. I'm enjoying an abundance
of warmth to replace my fear of the cold. Go figure.

Relighting the Torch

At times our own light goes out and is rekindled by a spark from another person. Each of us has cause to think with deep gratitude of those who have lighted the flame within us.

— ALBERT SCHWEITZER

I have never had the chance to thank some of the people who have jumpstarted my life when I needed it most. An art teacher who taught me to play guitar, my godmother who knew I was in love. Who are your people? A parent? A character in a movie? A stranger? Even a pet? They may not even know what they have done for you, and maybe it's not something that bears directly thanking them. We can still give thanks in a profound way for the facets of our lives that simply would never be possible without these singular, special people.

Gratitude functions best when amplified through action. Even if I never do get back in touch with that teacher, I have a chance to pass that spark of creativity to someone else who might be aching for it. I have a chance to spread the flame in me to others who feel like they're just going to smolder and sputter forever. When my spark goes out again one day, as I'm sure it will, I can trust that someone will come through and help me reignite it.

Our own bright flame can light the way for others.

Sweet Harvest

Gratitude is the fairest blossom which springs from the soul.

— HENRY WARD BEECHER

Toward the end of a long winter, a garden lover gets that itch. While the days are still too short and the ground still too frozen, the devoted get out their grow lights and their seed beds. Whether it's flowers, pumpkins, or everything in between, it is a gardener's great joy and love to prep and fuss from the beginning to the sweet end, and then start all over again in a glorious cycle that mirrors and builds on the one in the natural world.

Giving thanks in tiny ways, produce big yields.

We can always tend the gratitude in our hearts. Even when we're in an emotionally barren wasteland, when it feels like the light will never stick around long enough and there is no hope for those first green shoots, we have to keep our faith. Gratitude is a hardy stalk; it can sprout with almost no tending. Give it even half a chance by just murmuring something simple and mundane, at least once a day. "Thanks for pizza." "Thanks for sharp pencils." "Thanks for comfortable shoes." You don't have to do anything big, just help that gratitude push its way out of the seed and up into the light. You'll be amazed at how fast it sprouts and grows, and how beautifully it blossoms.

Gift Giving

Not what we say about our blessings, but how we use them, is the true measure of our thanksgiving.

— W.T. PURKISER

Using our gifts, whatever they may be, is the surest way to shout our praise.

I'm sure you've heard the saying "With great power comes great responsibility." I would also add that with great gifts come great responsibilities. Whether we're blessed with exceptional talents, abundant resources, or wonderful bursts of energy, the best way to thank the universe for sending them our way is to use them in service of something greater than ourselves. We can pray and intone and shout out our thanks as often as we like, and believe me there's nothing wrong with that, but as with many things the message comes across loudest through action.

It's much easier to talk about being thankful for what we have. In fact, we may even be able to talk ourselves into feeling that we're more grateful than we really are. We know we should feel lucky to have a roof over our heads and plenty of food to eat when we know there are so many who live in ongoing need. But we still, secretly, think we don't really have enough and wish we had more, and we feel a bit guilty about that. Spending a day a month in a soup kitchen or building a new home drives our gratitude home in a concrete, physical way. We come back to our home and family able to more truly appreciate what we have.

Its Own Reward

Act with kindness, but do not expect gratitude.

— Confucius

There is much to be said for uncomplicated motivations. Less is more. Do what you mean and mean what you do. There's no point in cluttering up a perfectly good gesture with a bunch of excess expectations.

I'm always impressed by parents who manage to bring up children who have a sense that they can and should do good things without the promise of a reward. It's very tempting to offer something in return. Clean your room and you'll get dessert; bring home a good report card and we'll go on a special trip. It's tempting because it works in an immediate sort of way, but the long-term effects aren't worth the trouble. The belief that every good deed or positive effort deserves a reward diminishes the intrinsic reward of being kind, doing for others, or achieving goals. Those things can and should feel good all by themselves. The desserts and the special trips can be enjoyed even more if they are spontaneous reasons to come together as a family and have a good time, unfettered by the expectations of tit for tat.

We can enjoy doing good for others with no anticipation of reward in return.

Surviving the Storm

The unthankful heart discovers no mercies; but the thankful heart will find, in every hour, some heavenly blessings.

— HENRY WARD BEECHER

Gratitude is free to anyone who claims it.

In reading or hearing about people who have suffered through great tragedy, I'm compelled by how they can remain so resilient. After going through hell on earth, they are still able to see the good in people, to notice small wonders, and, most amazingly, to be grateful. I don't know if I could ever be so strong—to get through something horrific and come out the other side not only alive but grateful, not only for the fact of my survival but for the experience itself.

I know I am blessed for not being directly touched by a great tragedy, which affords me a kind of naivety about it. From what I can guess, however, there is always good somehow within and around the bad. Someone who has lost the ability to be thankful might not be able to see those good things very easily or clearly, but they are there for the heart who can remain open to the possibility that they are there.

In more normal times, we can learn a huge lesson from these survivors. There is no moment or situation or difficulty that does not contain at least a tiny blessing in it, and we can always be on the lookout for that bit of solace.

Everyday Devotion

The ordinary acts we practice every day at home are of more importance to the soul than their simplicity might suggest.

— THOMAS MOORE

Does flossing your teeth feed your soul? Does sorting laundry make you thrive? It most certainly can. It's not just prayer that brings us closer to our spiritual selves. We don't turn off our soul's work in order to do the dishes. Any action at all can be devotional in nature if it is done from a clear, loving place. Caring for your body, your home, and your family don't have to be time away spiritual practice. They can be meditative, or they can just be what they are: simple actions, repeated, toward a goal of living better. The more positive energy we bring to them, the easier they will be and the more they will serve us on many levels.

We leave spiritual footprints through everyday intentions and actions.

I just saw a photograph of an elderly monk's bare feet standing next to the impression made by his own feet in the wood where he has stood to pray for over half a century. I gasped at the power of simplicity. Nothing but standing and praying, repeated every day, and the man's imprint was worn into the wood forever. It made me remember that we are making that same imprint, though it may not be so symbolically visible, every day as we go about our business.

Change It Up

The less routine the more life.

— AMOS BRONSON ALCOTT

"Has your daily life become a drag? Tired of the same old same old? Giving up on the grind? Come to Hawaii! (or, if you already live there, to Alaska!)"

Okay, so maybe you can't jet off tomorrow to an exotic locale and forget all your troubles. You can, however, ease up on a bit of the monotonous routine that we all get trapped in from time to time. You can make a big change like finding a new job or remodeling the kitchen, or it can be a small change, and I mean a really tiny one. Researchers say that even something as simple as brushing your teeth with your non-dominant hand can stimulate your brain into new kinds of activity. Driving a new route to the same old job may get you there feeling more renewed than yesterday. Trying a new food or learning a new sport can open up pathways in your brain that are lying dormant.

Doing the same thing day in and day out can make anyone feel limp and lifeless. You can grab hold of your life by stepping out of that sameness.

Break free of the doldrums with some simple changes to your regular routine.

115

Your True Self

Would that you could meet the sun and the wind with more of your body and less of your raiment.

— KAHLIL GIBRAN

I didn't know that raiment meant clothing until I just looked it up. Now I'm envisioning this quote emblazoned across the front gate of a nudist colony. It would seem to be the perfect naturalist's credo: get your naked body out of those confining shirts and pants and dresses and into the sun and wind. Or maybe it could be an advertisement for skimpy bikinis.

And if it's neither of the above, then let's go with the metaphorical: our natural state is the best way to experience our natural environment. No, it doesn't mean you have to strip down and run through the forest (ouch! pine cones!), but it does invite you to peel off the outer layers of propriety, correctness, even respectability. Those can all be good things, sure, but if you can find a way to face the elements with a bit more of your inner self you might be surprised at the result. You may find that all the outer garments you layer on to fit in might be at the very least confining and at most downright stifling.

Feel free to face the world with a bit more of your true self on display.

Love in All Things, Great and Small

I can do no great things, only small things with great love.

— MOTHER TERESA

When I read about the life stories of people I admire, like Mother Teresa, I am sometimes halted by a feeling that I can never live up to that kind of great achievement. How can I, when it seems like so often any prolonged attempt or grand plan inevitably hits a road block and falters? I have to remember it's only in retrospect that anyone's life takes on the look of a magnificent triumph. Under the microscope, no single day or separate action can ever bear that weight. It is the alchemy of greatness to string those things together into a wonderful whole.

Less doing, more loving.

I don't have to aspire to greatness in my everyday actions. In fact if I do I'm more likely to fail than not. Constantly thinking about trying to be great or do great things is like trying to harvest seedlings—quite a few important steps are being skipped in the process, and the perspective is all wrong. Instead of planning a great end product, our energies are best spent in careful attention to the here and now. To bringing our talents and enthusiasm to each task in its turn. To doing the right thing at the right moment. To doing the things we can do, brimming over with the most love we can muster.

The Starting Line

Happiness is itself a kind of gratitude.

— J O S E P H   W O O D   K R U T C H

Gratitude and happiness feed each other, growing together in a wonderful symbiosis.

In order to be happy, we often feel we must deserve it, as though happiness were some kind of end of the year bonus at work, something we toil away for and can sort of expect if we've done things as we feel we ought to do them. I say *phooey!* You and I and the lady next door have the unconditional right to be happy. Right now. It need not be deserved, it need not be earned.

I'll let you in on a little secret: happiness is not the ending place we have made it out to be in our minds. Happiness is not the finish line, it's the starting block. We can't wait for our lives to change in order to find happiness, we must find happiness in order for our lives to change. And the clearest path to happiness that I know is gratitude.

A daily practice of gratitude helps us set aside some of those stubborn obstacles to our happiness: bitterness, depression, lack of what we feel we want or need. That same "attitude of gratitude" quite handily brings us what we do need to make us happier: clarity of purpose, inspiration, and abundance.

What You Already Know

I finally figured out the only reason to be alive is to enjoy it.

— RITA MAE BROWN

You wake up, your eyelids stuck shut. You ramble through your morning routine, cursing under your breath. Caffeine helps. A shower helps a little more. Then you're finally ready to face (sigh) another day.

How did things get to be this way? Or better, how did you get to be this way? You wonder if there was ever a time when you didn't feel so shut down, fearful, crazed, and diminished. Maybe certain times as a kid. Maybe playing music or a game of soccer or chess.

Life can be a playground. We wake up on a planet more diverse, more exciting, more unknown than any we could hope to imagine. We can wake up to endless possibility each and every morning, and yet more often than not we wake up to the crushing push of our limitations. We spend all day trying to bend the "I cant's" into "I'll try's" and hoping for the best. It may be that all we need is a single "I will." It can be one of your choosing, something like:

I will enjoy it.
I will laugh through it.
I will bless it up, down and sideways.

Never again ask yourself why you are alive. You already know. Enjoy it.

To Our Readers

Conari Press, an imprint of Red Wheel/Weiser, publishes books on topics ranging from spirituality, personal growth, and relationships to women's issues, parenting, and social issues. Our mission is to publish quality books that will make a difference in people's lives—how we feel about ourselves and how we relate to one another. We value integrity, compassion, and receptivity, both in the books we publish and in the way we do business.

Our readers are our most important resource, and we value your input, suggestions, and ideas about what you would like to see published. Please feel free to contact us, to request our latest book catalog, or to be added to our mailing list.

Conari Press
An imprint of Red Wheel/Weiser, LLC
500 Third Street, Suite 230
San Francisco, CA 94107
www.redwheelweiser.com

Dedicated to Louise Rosen

Special thanks to Samantha Soule, Denis Butkus, Julie Kline, Stephen Willems, Jack Doulin, Wendy vanden Heuvel, Lila Blue Coley, Kathryn Kates, David Adjmi, Margaret Welshons, Mary Pat Flandrick, Sarah Grace Wilson, Sean Dugan, Daniel Reitz, Crystal Skillman, Martin and Rochelle Denton, Jan Leslie and Chayda Harding, Kirsten Kelly, Joel Moritz, Dayna Jean, Brett and Cameron Talbott, Jeremy Sparks, Brandi Davis, Shana and Kayla Kendrick, Mattie and Bill Tirey, Robert and Louise Rosen, Darlene Rodrigues, Denise Reber, Ardie Kendrick, Jean and Susie Pral, Jan Johnson, and Bailey Drew Talbott.